Drawing Is Easy

DRAWING WITH
Objects

GODELEINE DE ROSAMEL

Gareth Stevens Publishing
A WORLD ALMANAC EDUCATION GROUP COMPANY

Please visit our web site at: www.garethstevens.com
For a free color catalog describing Gareth Stevens Publishing's list
of high-quality books and multimedia programs, call 1-800-542-2595 (USA) or
1-800-387-3178 (Canada). Gareth Stevens Publishing's fax: (414) 332-3567.

Library of Congress Cataloging-in-Publication Data

De Rosamel, Godeleine.
    [Dessine avec des objets. English]
    Drawing with objects/by Godeleine De Rosamel.
      p. cm. — (Drawing is easy)
    Summary: Step-by-step illustrations demonstrate how to use outlines of familiar objects
as the starting point for drawings.
    Includes bibliographical references.
    ISBN 0-8368-3627-8 (lib. bdg.)
    1. Drawing—Technique—Juvenile literature. [1. Drawing—Technique.] I. Title.
NC655.R66813   2003
741.2—dc21   2002036536

This edition first published in 2003 by
Gareth Stevens Publishing
A World Almanac Education Group Company
330 West Olive Street, Suite 100
Milwaukee, WI 53212 USA

This edition © 2003 by Gareth Stevens, Inc.
First published as *Dessine: Avec des objets* in 2001 by Editions Casterman.
© 2001 by Casterman. Additional end matter © 2003 by Gareth Stevens, Inc.

Translation: Patrice Lantier
Gareth Stevens editor: Dorothy L. Gibbs
Gareth Stevens designer: Melissa Valuch
Cover design: Melissa Valuch

Printed in the United States of America

1 2 3 4 5 6 7 8 9 07 06 05 04 03

Table of Contents

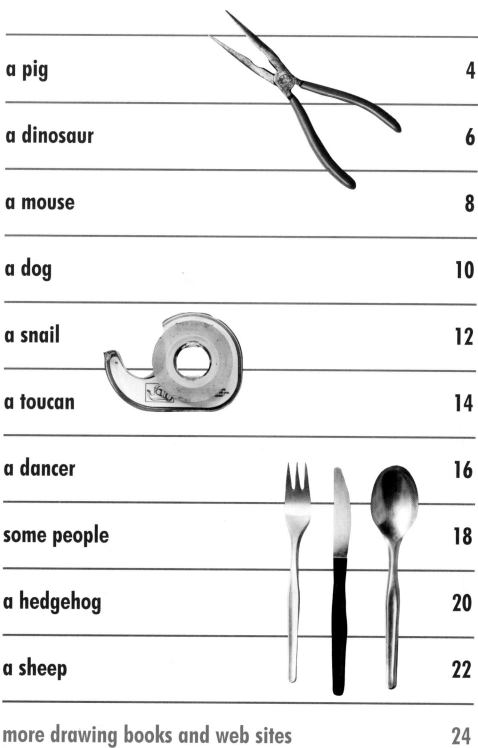

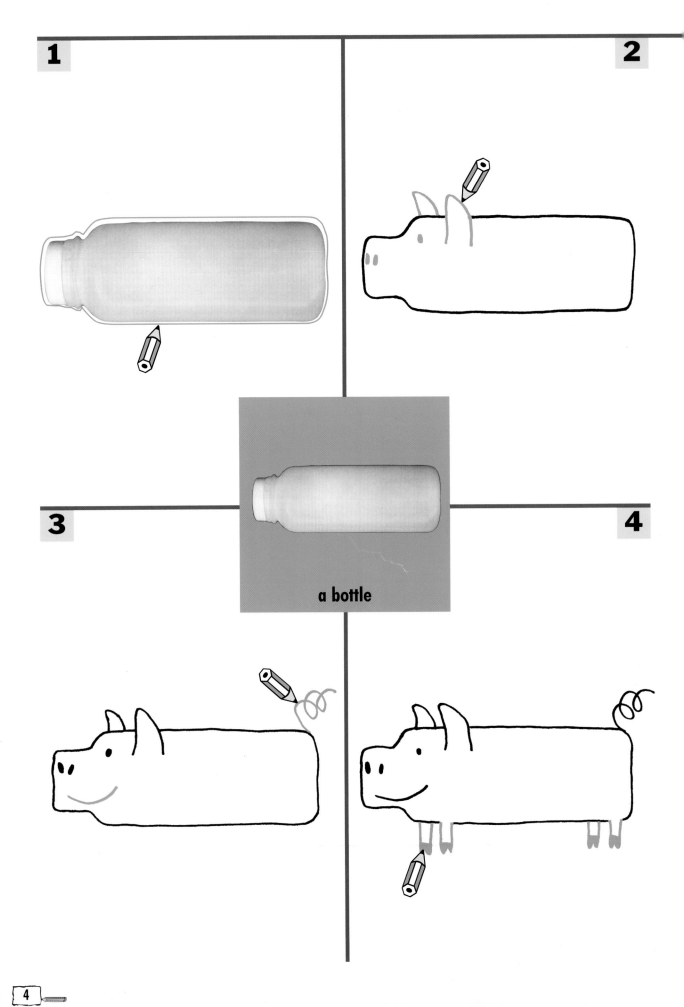

1

2

3

a bottle

4

a pig

vitamin bottle

glue bottle

juice bottle

a papa pig **a baby pig** **a mama pig**

1

2

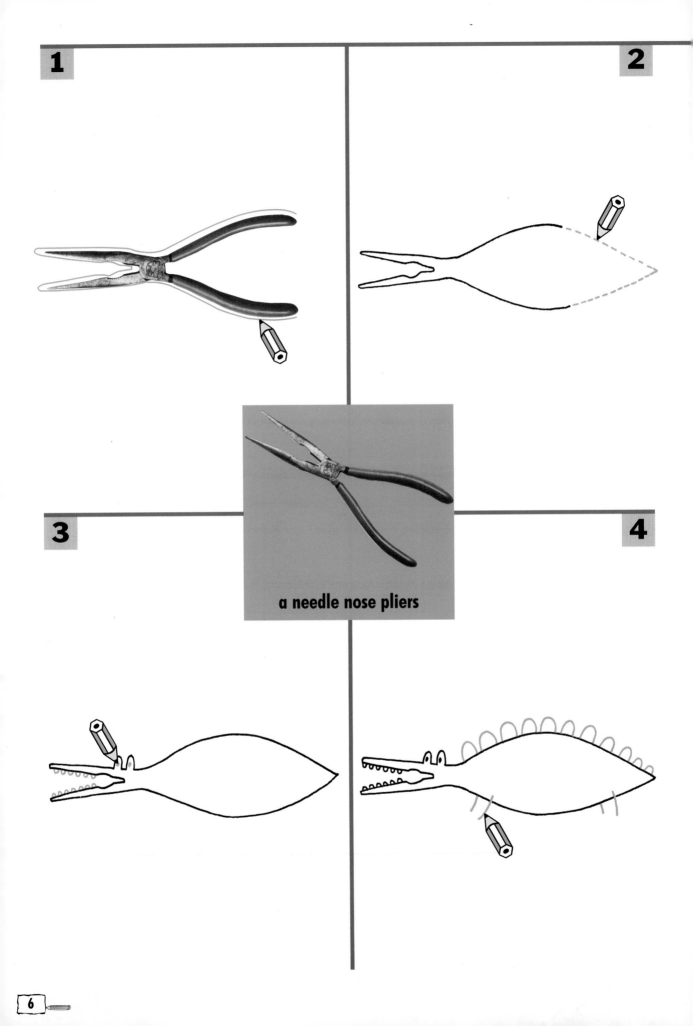

a needle nose pliers

3

4

a dinosaur

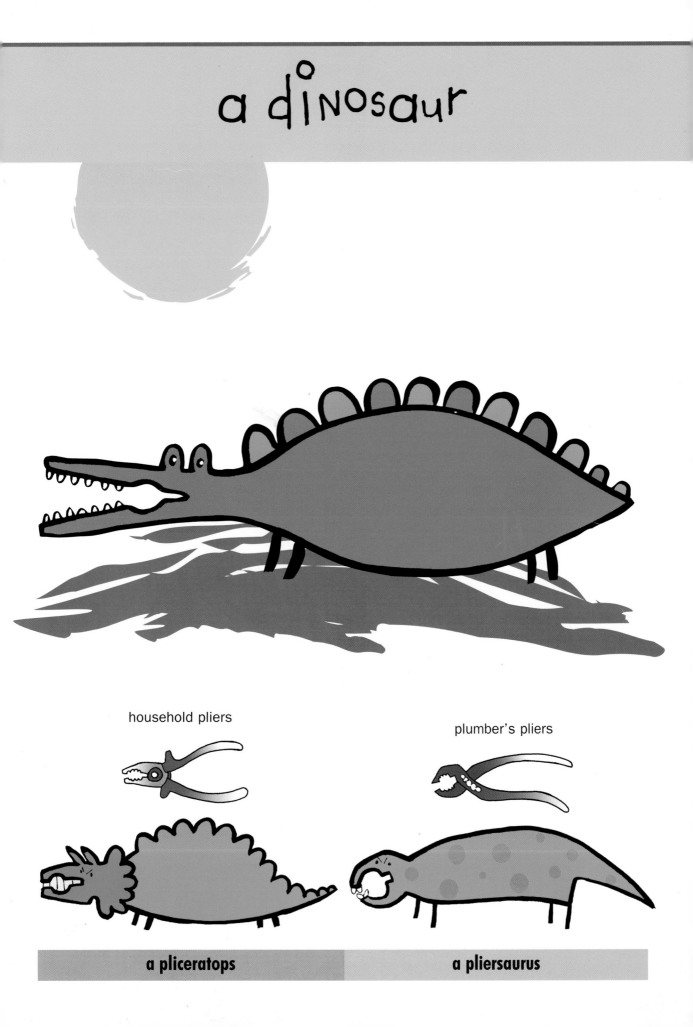

household pliers

plumber's pliers

a pliceratops

a pliersaurus

1

2

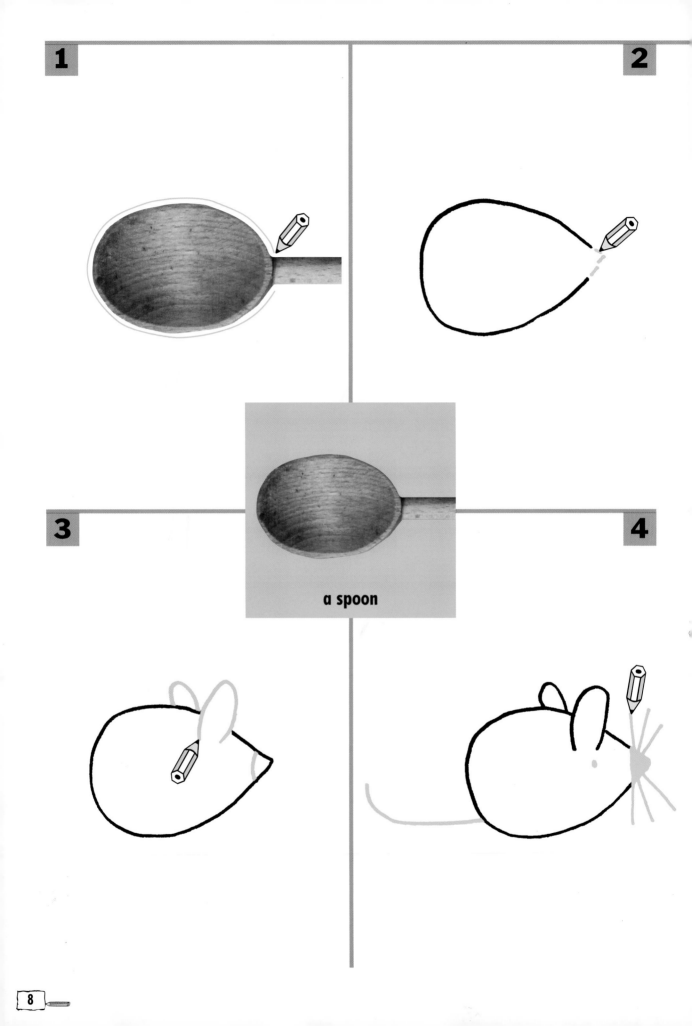

a spoon

3

4

a mouse

a mole   a hamster   a ladybug

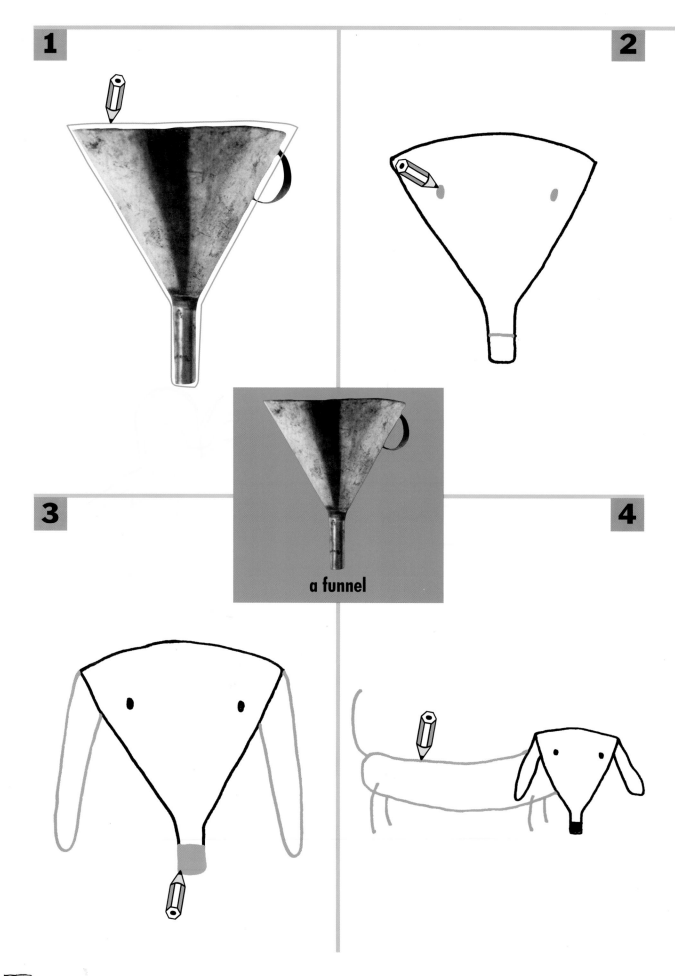

1

2

a funnel

3

4

a dog

| a watchdog | a dog face | a playful dog |

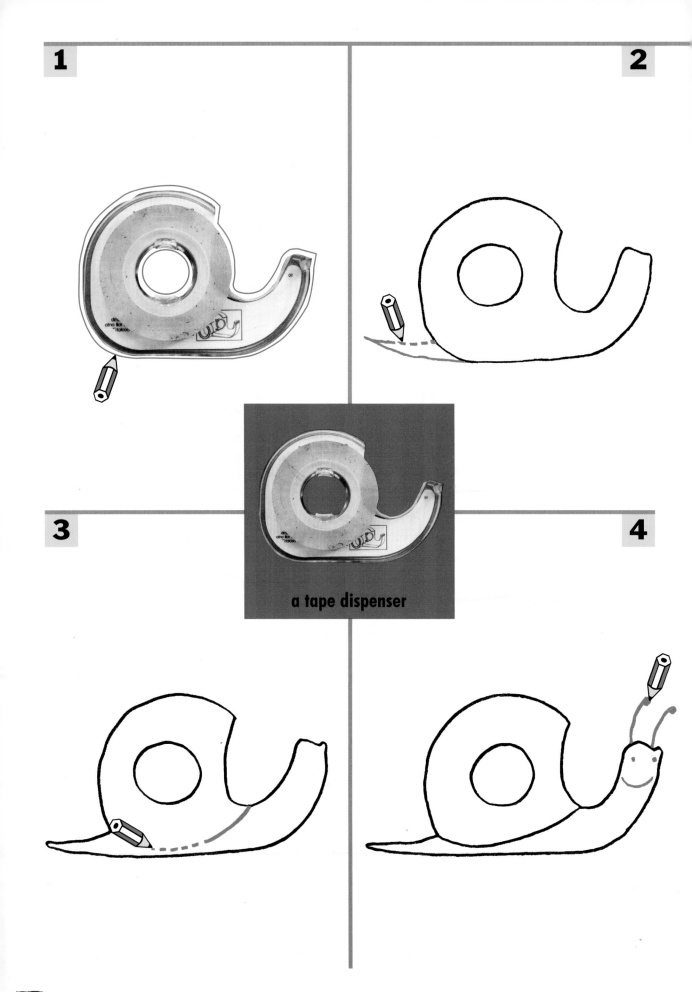

1

2

a tape dispenser

3

4

a snail

| a penguin | a whale | a helicopter |

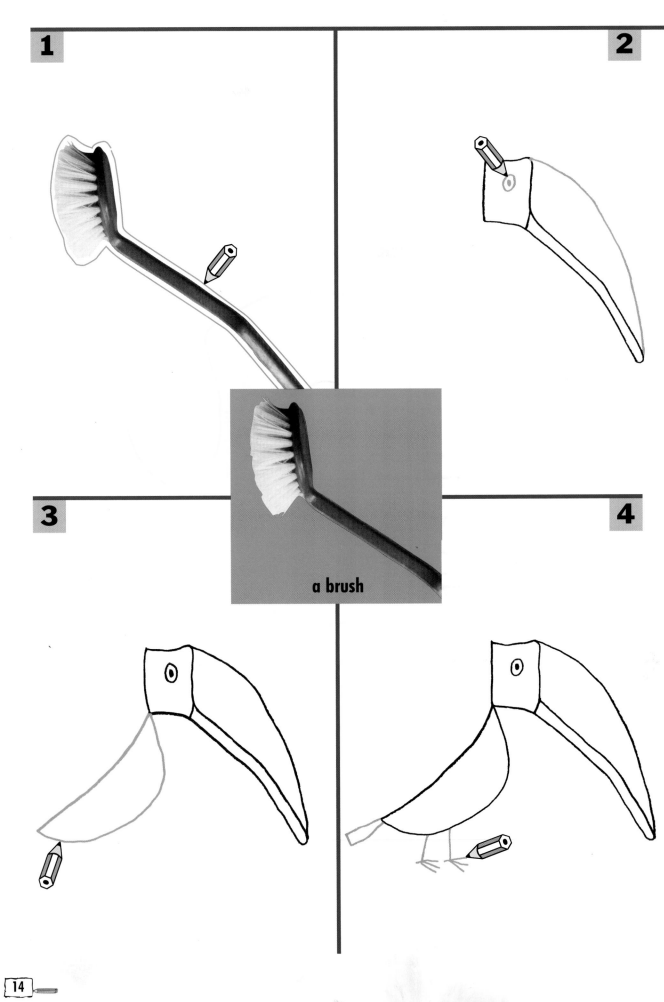

1

2

a brush

3

4

a toucan

a heron

a giraffe

1

2

a glass

3

4

a dancer

a ballroom dancer   **a dancing princess**   **a ballerina**

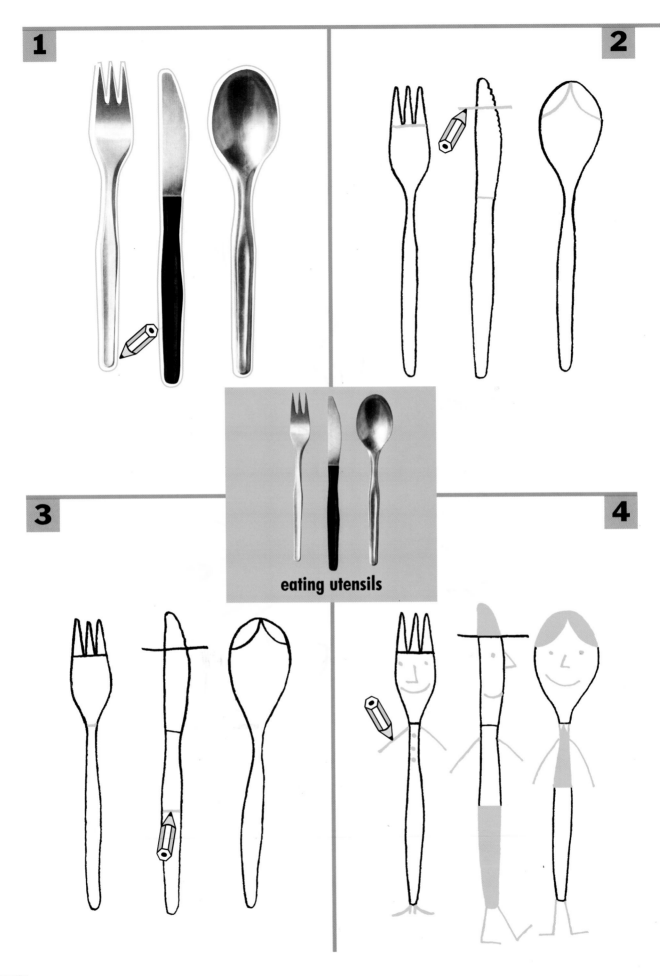

eating utensils

some people

cheese slicer

small strainer

salad tongs

a girl   **a boy**   **a man**

1 Dip the brush into watercolor paint.

2 Press the brush onto a sheet of thick paper or a piece of cardboard.

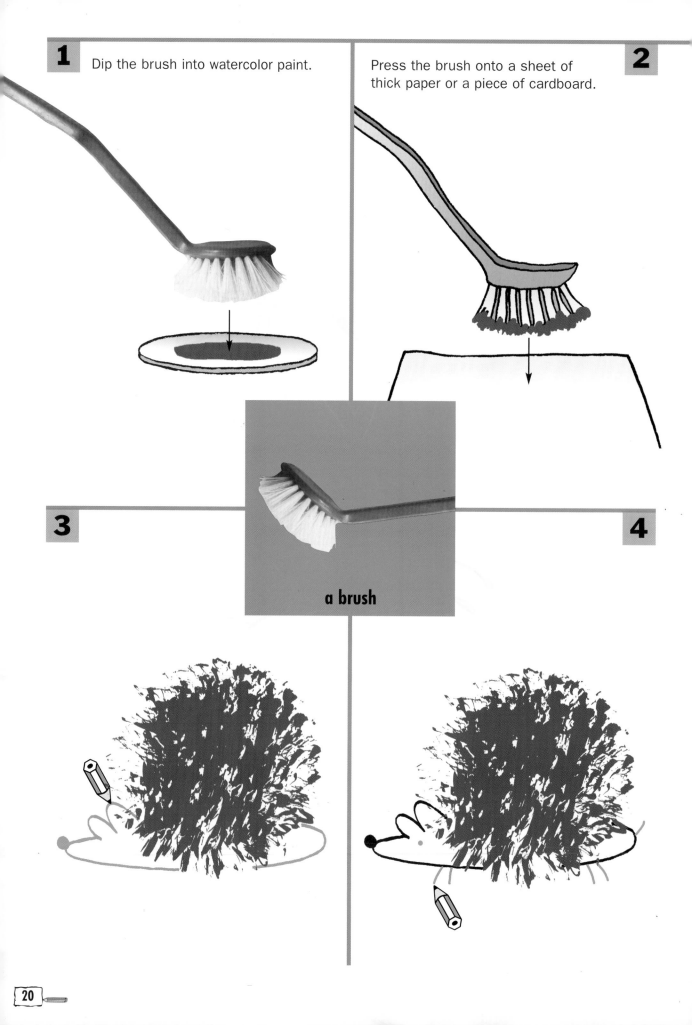

a brush

3

4

a hedgehog

a dandelion   **a bear**   **an ostrich**

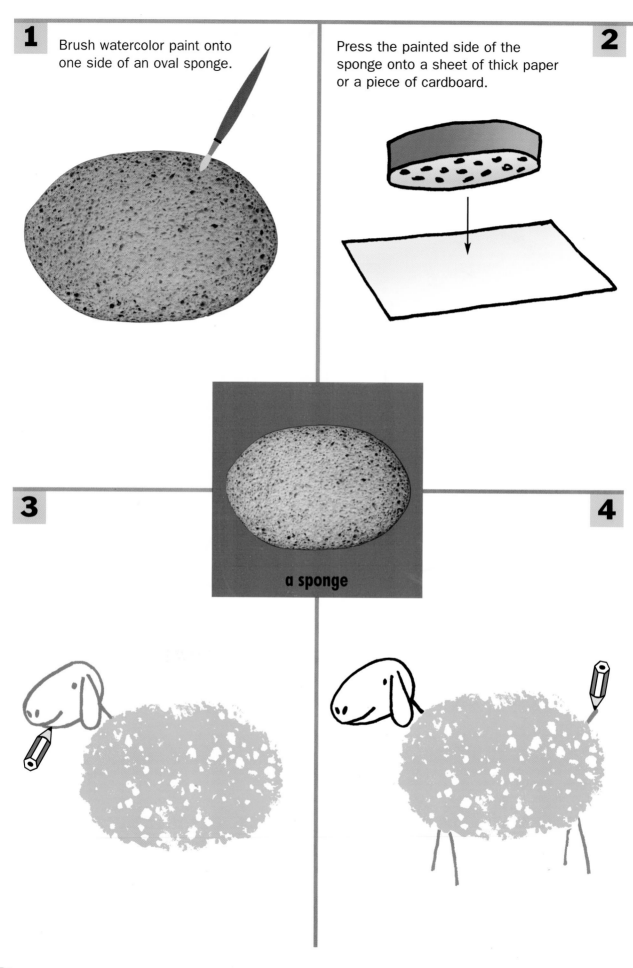

1 Brush watercolor paint onto one side of an oval sponge.

2 Press the painted side of the sponge onto a sheet of thick paper or a piece of cardboard.

a sponge

3

4

a sheep

a goat

a ram

more drawing books

- *Build a Doodle 1*
  Beverly Armstrong
  (Learning Works)

- *How to Draw Dinosaurs. Art Smart* (series)
  Christine C. Smith
  (Gareth Stevens)

- *Let's Start! Stenciling*
  (Silver Dolphin)

web sites

- 4Kids2Play: Colouring
  4kids2play.nl/eng

- How to draw Chunky Monkey®
  www.chunkymonkey.com/howto/howtodrawcm.htm